SAVING
WHITE
SHARKS

. . . it's not what we have to fear from white sharks,
but rather what we have to fear for them.

INTRODUCTION

When I sat down more than 30 years ago to write *Jaws*, I had a lot of freedom as a storyteller. At the time, virtually nothing was known about the lives of white sharks—or most other sharks for that matter. In the absence of scientific knowledge, I was free to tell a tale in which white sharks attack boats (which we now know they don't do) and attack and eat people (which we've since learned they don't really like to do).

In the years since *Jaws* was published, our understanding of white sharks has grown immeasurably. So, too, has our awareness of the serious threats sharks face around the world. The populations of some shark species have declined by 90 percent because of overfishing. Globally, it's estimated that more than 100 million sharks are killed each year by commercial fishing fleets—half in fisheries targeting sharks, half as accidental catch in gear intended for other species.

White sharks are also the targets of a worldwide trophy trade, a threat so serious that just weeks ago they were granted protection through the Convention on International Trade in Endangered Species of Flora and Fauna.

If we are to live in a world with white sharks, we must learn more about their lives and learn to appreciate them as the magnificent animals that they are. And we must take steps to protect them in the wild. I'm delighted that the Monterey Bay Aquarium is contributing on all fronts.

Aquarium staff and their research colleagues are studying white sharks, using electronic tags to track the movements of juvenile and adult white sharks as they swim through the

"Imagine . . . this little girl shark in the Outer Bay will grow up to be like this!" —Peter Benchley. An adult white shark may reach 21 feet and could weigh 7,000 pounds. The average shark is closer to 15 feet.

Fewer than 30 people a year are attacked by sharks of all species worldwide—far more are killed by bee stings.

ocean. They're also able to study the growth and development of a young white shark on exhibit—the first time anyone has been able to monitor the growth and development of a young white shark. What we'll learn from this work will be information essential to protecting white sharks in the wild.

The aquarium is also helping thousands of people learn to see white sharks with new eyes. I've seen and dived with white sharks many times in the wild, and it's always an inspiring experience. In the same way, it was a treat to visit the aquarium for its 20th anniversary and to watch a young white shark swimming just inches away, together with tunas, sea turtles and other animals in the Outer Bay exhibit. I was thrilled by the opportunity to spend time with her, and to hear the excitement and appreciation that other visitors expressed about being in her presence.

I'm glad that public attitudes toward sharks are changing. Today, three decades removed from *Jaws*, I work on books and films designed to raise awareness about the threats facing ocean wildlife, and what each of us can do to help.

Together, we can assure a future where white sharks roam the seas.

Peter Benchley
Princeton, New Jersey
October 22, 2004

"We fear shark attacks, but sharks aren't trying to eat you, they're biting to see what you are. Seven out of ten people bitten by white sharks survive." —Benchley

SAVING WHITE SHARKS

"If there's one thing I'm dead certain of, it's that I could not write Jaws *today. I could not turn this beautiful beast into a villain."*

Peter Benchley, author of *Jaws*

White sharks may well be the most fascinating and misunderstood animals in the ocean. The myths surrounding them have done nothing to help protect these threatened creatures however. Their ancestors swam the seas when dinosaurs roamed the shores and sharks have survived eons of change on Earth. But they may not survive us. Their future is uncertain, and their fate may be extinction. We must quickly learn more about white sharks to better manage and protect wild populations.

While studying them in their natural habitat is essential, it also poses immense challenges. That's why the Monterey Bay Aquarium has been keeping a young female white shark alive in the Outer Bay exhibit as part of its white shark research program. Since settling into her new home on September 14, 2004, she has lived longer than in any previous attempt

worldwide, and is doing well as of this writing. Her presence is helping both scientists and visitors alike learn more about these mysterious and maligned creatures in the wild.

"White sharks are the myth of our age ... extraordinary, large, swift, perfect in every way," National Geographic photographer David Doubilet tells a large crowd of aquarium visitors who have come to see her.

As she glides around the million-gallon exhibit using occasional bursts of speed, the young shark steers clear of the 300-pound giant bluefin tuna on her right, or the Galapagos and hammerhead sharks circling below. She is the only white shark on exhibit anywhere in the world.

About five feet long and weighing some 70 pounds, this months-old juvenile female is

The young female took readily to her new home in the Outer Bay exhibit, sometimes gliding in a long path, or swimming fast and making quick turns along the back wall.

the perfect mini-version of the adult "great" white shark demonized in *Jaws* and other mainstream media. That was before we knew better.

"These animals are so sophisticated. We've learned so much. It's almost as if it's not the same animal that I wrote about 30 years ago," says author Peter Benchley, after watching her navigate the Outer Bay exhibit.

Seeing her firsthand has already given hundreds of thousands of people a personal encounter with a living, breathing white shark, inspiring them and engaging their help in protecting these animals in the wild. Once visitors see her, fear is quickly replaced by fascination.

"Bringing people face to face with living marine animals is a powerful way to move them to care about the oceans and ocean life," says Cynthia Vernon, the aquarium's vice president of conservation programs. "We believe there is no better way for us to raise the awareness about the threats white sharks face than to let people see for themselves what magnificent and fascinating animals they are, to tell the story of the threats they face in the wild, and offer ways to take action that will protect white sharks."

"It's great to see aquarium visitors treating her like a wonder, asking that she be taken care of, making sure she's OK," remarks Benchley. "Having a great white shark here is an unprecedented opportunity to learn things that have never been known about these animals."

As she would in the open sea, the young shark eats fish several times a week. She dines primarily on salmon fillets and vitamin-enriched mackerel. She's gaining weight steadily, and

hasn't yet threatened her exhibit-mates. As she grows older, her diet will likely change. In the wild she'd begin hunting red meat in the form of sea lions and seals, or scavenge blubber from a dead whale. Sharks need large amounts of rich protein for the energy to elevate their body temperatures in cooler seas, and to fuel high-speed ambushes on unsuspecting prey.

The young female came from the warmer waters

How do you feed a white shark? Aquarists attach wild-caught salmon and mackerel to the tip of a long bamboo pole several times a week when she shows signs of interest in feeding. If at any time the young shark isn't doing well, she could be released back into the wild. And when she outgrows the exhibit, she'll be tagged and released where she was caught, giving researchers even more insights into the lives of white sharks.

Aquarium biologists monitor the young shark around the clock, feeding her as much wild-caught salmon and mackerel as she wants.

off the coast of Southern California, a region scientists suspect is a nursery ground for white sharks. We don't know where she was born. Her mother may have given birth to up to fourteen live young, each several feet long. The baby sharks immediately swam away, on their own from the start, swimming off into a black hole of knowledge on our part. Where do they spend

time? How far do they travel? How deep do they dive? What eats young white sharks, if anything? We still know frustratingly little about them. By studying the young female here, and tagging and following others in the wild, we're helping fill in the knowledge gaps.

To help create better informed shark conservation policy and raise public awareness about the plight of all shark species, the aquarium launched its multi-year white shark research program in 2002, and is currently partnering with researchers around the world to study several species of ocean predators in the Tagging of Pacific Pelagics program. Scientists are studying these animals in the wild to better understand their complex lives. Electronic

OPPOSITE: *Biologists placed the young white shark in a four-million-gallon pen off the coast of Malibu to help her recover from the stress and injury of being caught in a fisherman's gill net.* ABOVE: *Small enough to be scooped up in a handnet, she was carefully placed in a stretcher and carried to a 3,000-gallon mobile life support transport.*

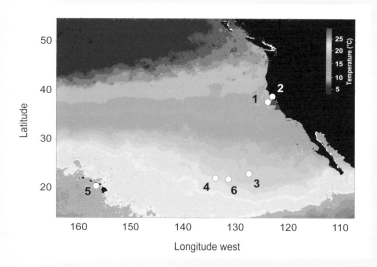

STUDYING WHITE SHARKS IN THE WILD

At the Tuna Research and Conservation Center (TRCC), a collaboration between Stanford University and the Monterey Bay Aquarium, scientists are tagging and studying young white sharks year-round, and adult white sharks at the Farallon Islands off San Francisco. Tagged adults have turned up as far west as Hawaii, revealing that white sharks make long-distance oceanic migrations.

TRCC researchers are also tagging other sharks in the North Pacific as part of a multi-year, multi-institution collaboration called Tagging of Pacific Pelagics (TOPP). TOPP brings together scientists from the U.S., Canada, Mexico, Japan and the United Kingdom. Together

they're studying the migration patterns of large, open-ocean animals, like white sharks, bluefin tuna, elephant seals, albatrosses, sea turtles, whales and other marine species in the North Pacific Ocean. For more information, visit www.toppcensus.org.

Others partners in white shark research include the Shark Lab at California State University, Long Beach, and the Southern California Marine Institute.

A Pop-off Satellite Archival Tag hitches a ride on a shark, collecting data on temperature, depth and light. On a preset date, the tag pops off the shark, bobs to the surface and sends data via satellite to the lab. Researchers were surprised when tagged sharks wandered far from the coast, and regularly dove deep, to nearly 2,000 feet. One shark traveled from California to Hawaii, spending six months in the warmer waters.

Release Area (Sept. 8th, 2003)
Popup Area (Nov. 7th, 2003)

Juvenile white sharks tagged off the coast of Southern California have been tracked as far south as Baja California. Map based on unpublished findings of Kevin Weng.

*Given the way white sharks have been demonized in popular culture,
a change in public attitude is critical if we want to assure their survival.*

tags let researchers "eavesdrop" on the sharks, revealing where they go, how deep they swim and the water temperatures they prefer.

"Our current tagging and research efforts with sharks are complemented with this white shark on exhibit, allowing people to see how white sharks behave and feed more naturally, instead of from inside a cage with movie lights glaring at them. . . . The more we learn, the more we will be able to help manage and conserve the wild population," notes Dr. John McCosker, shark expert and chair of aquatic biology at the California Academy of Sciences.

In the first two years of the aquarium's white shark program, scientists tagged and released four young white sharks, tracking them for a total of 184 days and recording migrations as far down as the Baja Peninsula. In 2003, aquarium biologists also held a young shark in an ocean pen for five days. Even in that short time, it fed before it was returned to the wild.

"We're beginning to shed some light on what these animals are doing," notes Dr. Randy

Kochevar, science communications manager with the aquarium. "Until now, their lives have been a great mystery."

What we're learning turns our fear of these vilified creatures inside out—it's not what we have to fear from them, but rather what we have to fear **for** them. We've hunted and netted this species to the point of endangerment in the wild. Without knowing that they are relatively few in number, slow to bear young, and widely distributed around the world, we've caught countless tons of

TOP: *Like thousands of others of its kind, a blue shark is caught in a fishing net intended for other species.* BOTTOM: *Children surround the jaws of a 22-foot white shark caught off the coast of South Africa, one of the first countries to protect white sharks in the wild.*

them. Many times sharks are caught unintentionally, and some fishermen are working with the aquarium to in its efforts to save sharks.

That's how the young female came to be here. She was accidentally entangled in a halibut gillnet by a commercial fisherman. Quick action by fishermen and staff taking part in the white shark research program saved her life. To help her recover from the stress of capture, she was placed in a four-million-gallon ocean pen off the coast of Malibu. Biologists watched her for a little over three weeks as she learned to navigate in an enclosed space. She appeared to be eating, either taking fish from lines lowered into the pen, or from schools of fish swimming within the net.

Healthy and stable, she was transported

Sharks are in trouble worldwide. More than 100 million sharks are killed each year, half of them victims of fishing gear seeking other species. Fishermen get a good price for shark fins, which are stripped off the animal while it's still alive. The rest of the shark is often thrown overboard to die, a practice illegal in the U.S.

SEAFOOD WATCH: CHOICES FOR HEALTHY OCEANS

To help protect white sharks and other fishes threatened by overfishing, or caught in ways that harm the environment, the aquarium launched **Seafood Watch**. Working with other aquariums and zoos, restaurants, universities, food co-ops, supermarkets and seafood suppliers among its many partners, Seafood Watch produces a convenient seafood guide for making wise choices when going to restaurants or grocery stores, giving everyone the power to help assure healthy oceans in the future. Learn more and download the latest Seafood Watch pocket guide at www.montereybayaquarium.org.

California is working on establishing a network of strategically placed marine protected areas that will help ensure the survival both of white sharks and many other species off our coast.

PROTECTING WHITE SHARKS

Some nations have already taken steps to protect white sharks in the wild—South Africa and Australia, among others. Recently, white sharks won worldwide trade protection from the Convention on International Trade in Endangered Species, a United Nations Treaty Organization. Trade in white sharks or their body parts is only allowed if it does not threaten the survival of the species. Of the 350 or so species of sharks thought to exist worldwide, the International Union for the Conservation of Nature lists 79 as imperiled, ranging from "critically endangered" to "near threatened." White sharks are considered "vulnerable." Like all sharks, white sharks play a vital role in the ocean's food web. They're top predators in the sea, but are in grave danger of being depleted

Due to overfishing (by-catch), trophy hunting and international market demand for sharks, white sharks have been deemed by World Wildlife Fund U.S. as "one of the 10 most likely species in the wild to go extinct soon."

to the aquarium's Outer Bay exhibit in a 3,000-gallon mobile life-support transport vehicle. She quickly adjusted to her new habitat, swimming easily around the exhibit and eating readily when offered food.

"We feed her until she stops eating," says Senior Aquarist Manny Ezcurra. "She ate more at first, but now she's gained weight and eats less often. Sometimes, she bites off the body of a whole mackerel we tie to the end of a long pole, leaving the head behind. Salmon fillets disappear entirely. It's so exciting, because caring for a shark like this has never been done before. She's doing so well because she came here healthy and strong."

Biologists monitor her around the clock. She'll remain in the exhibit as long as she does well. If the aquarium's veterinarian and staff aquarists determine that she won't adapt to the multi-species exhibit and she would survive if released, they may make the decision to return her to the wild.

The exhibiting of a white shark in Monterey is a major accomplishment in the aquarium's three-year project to study young white sharks off the coast of Southern California, and to determine whether it's possible to keep one on long-term exhibit. "This shark is the best ambassador that sharks could have," the aquarium's Vice President of Husbandry Randy Hamilton contends. "This single shark will truly help inspire people about the plight of all sharks in the wild."

This first-ever opportunity to study a living white shark as she grows up is offering both researchers and visitors an historic glimpse into the lives of this near-mythical species. It's also helping discover what we must do to stop the decline and even disappearance of white sharks worldwide.